Workbook

Number and Letter Tracing for Adult Students

This tool is designed to help adult students practice and master handwriting. It is appropriate for literacy, ESL, and ABE classes.

UPPERCASE

Trace the Letter. A

A A A A A A A

A A A A A A A

A A A A A A A

Lowercase

Trace the Letter. a

a a a a a a a a

a a a a a a a a

a a a a a a a a

UPPERCASE

Trace the Letter.

B

B B B B B B B

B B B B B B B

B B B B B B B

Lowercase

Trace the Letter.

b

b b b b b b b b b

b b b b b b b b b

b b b b b b b b b

UPPERCASE
Trace the Letter.
C
Lowercase
Trace the Letter.
c

UPPERCASE

Trace the Letter. D

D D D D D D
D D D D D D
D D D D D D

Lowercase

Trace the Letter. d

d d d d d d d d d
d d d d d d d d d
d d d d d d d d d

UPPERCASE

Trace the Letter.

E

Lowercase

Trace the Letter.

e

UPPERCASE
Trace the Letter.
F
Lowercase
Trace the Letter.
f

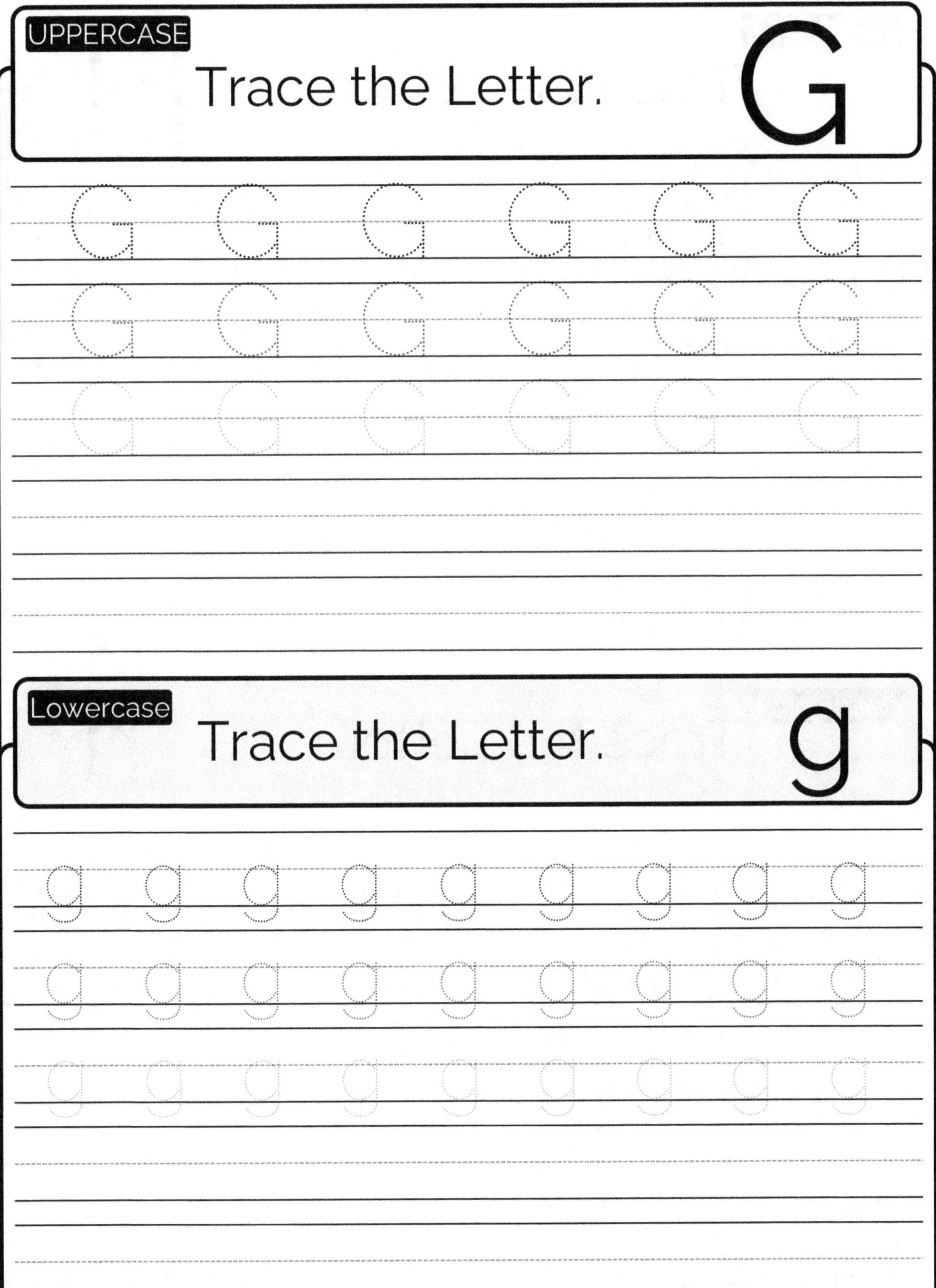
UPPERCASE
Trace the Letter.
G
Lowercase
Trace the Letter.
g

UPPERCASE

Trace the Letter.

H

Lowercase

Trace the Letter.

h

UPPERCASE
Trace the Letter.
I
Lowercase
Trace the Letter.
i

UPPERCASE
Trace the Letter.
J
Lowercase
Trace the Letter.
j

UPPERCASE
Trace the Letter.
K
Lowercase
Trace the Letter.
k

UPPERCASE

Trace the Letter. L

Lowercase

Trace the Letter. l

UPPERCASE

Trace the Letter. M

M M M M M M

M M M M M M

M M M M M M

Lowercase

Trace the Letter. m

m m m m m m m

m m m m m m m

m m m m m m m

UPPERCASE

Trace the Letter. N

Lowercase

Trace the Letter. n

UPPERCASE
Trace the Letter.
O
Lowercase
Trace the Letter.
o

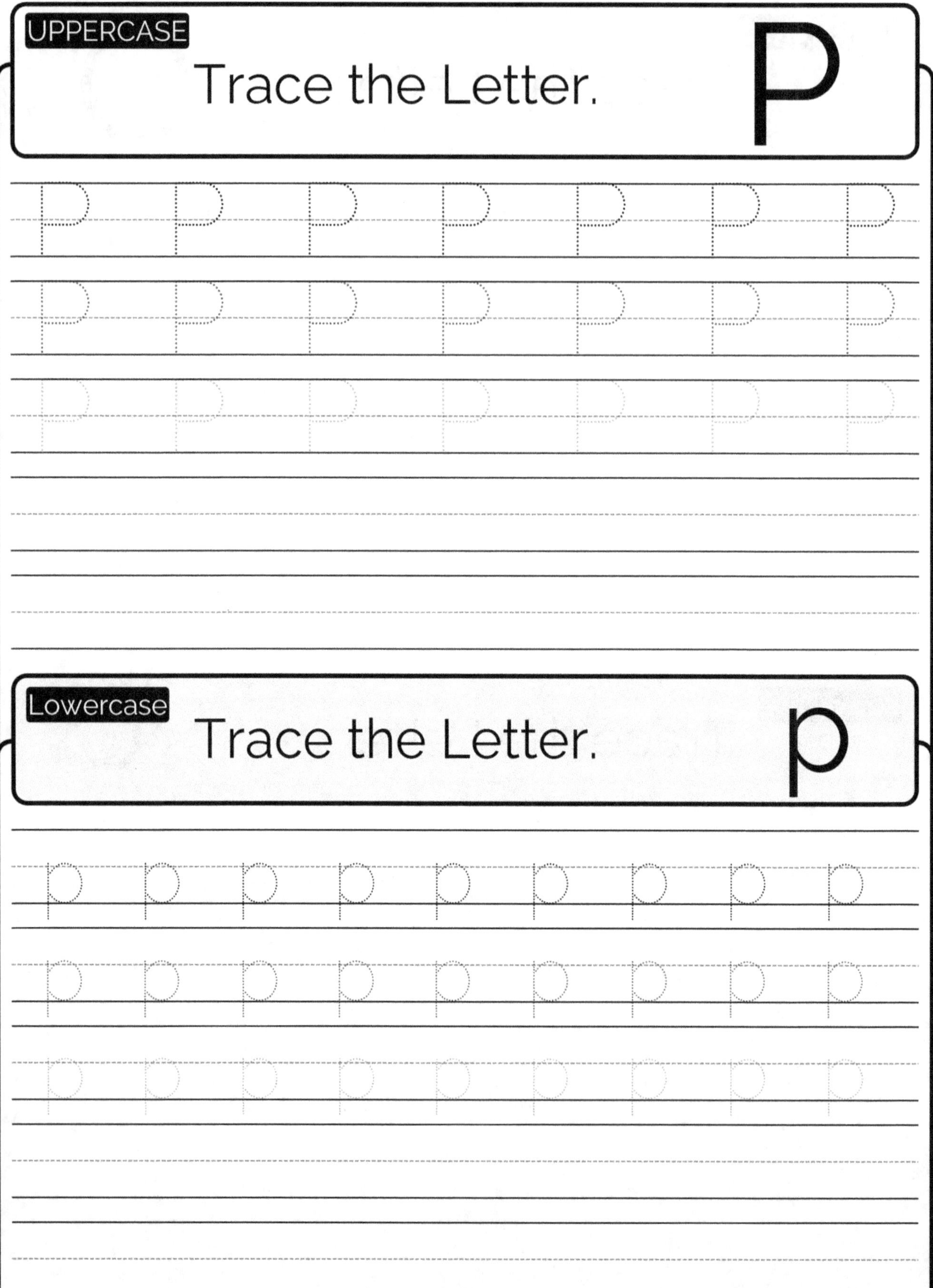
UPPERCASE
Trace the Letter.
P
Lowercase
Trace the Letter.
p

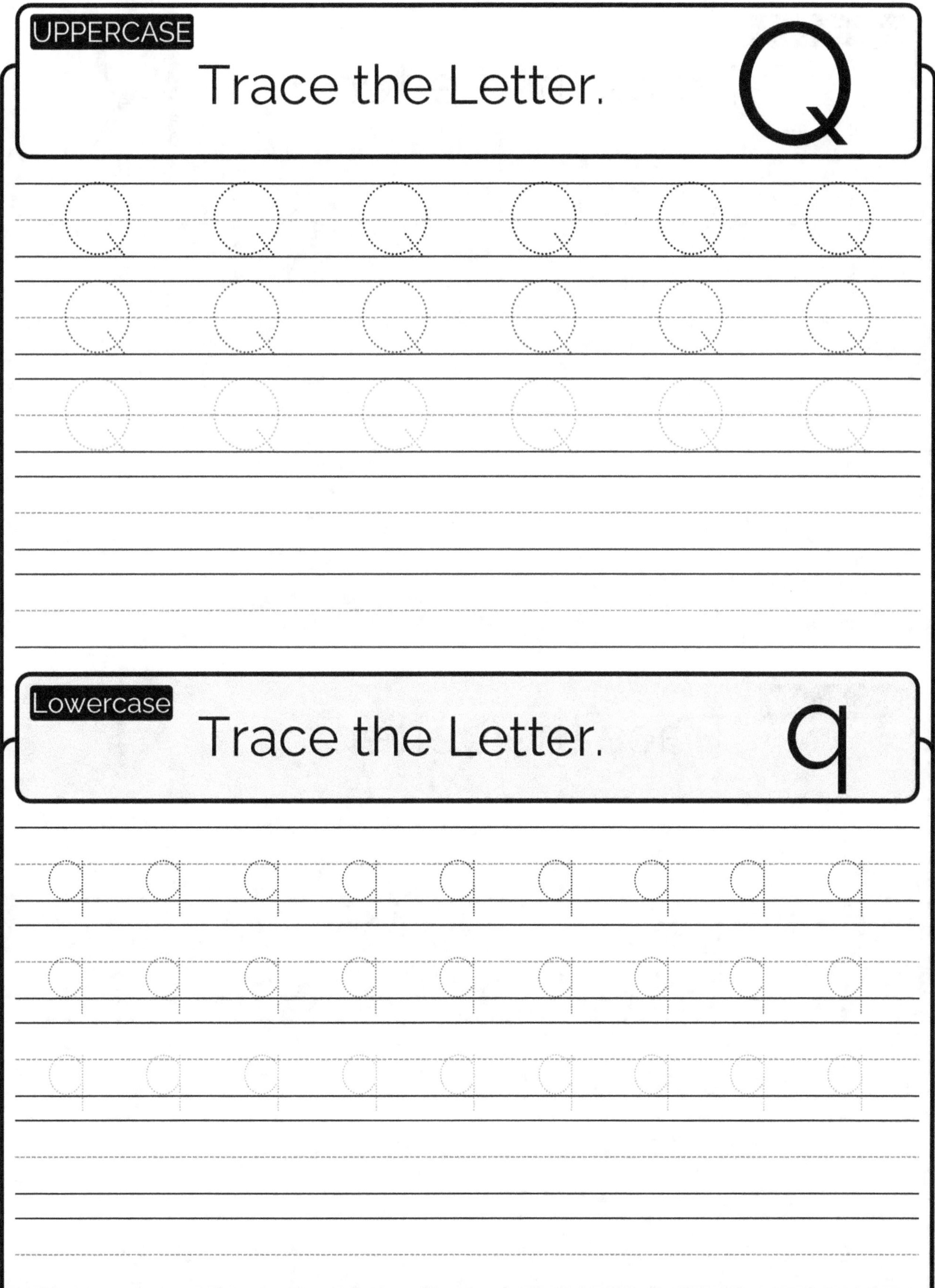

UPPERCASE
Trace the Letter.
Q
Lowercase
Trace the Letter.
q

UPPERCASE
Trace the Letter.
R
Lowercase
Trace the Letter.
r

UPPERCASE

Trace the Letter. S

S S S S S S S
S S S S S S S
S S S S S S S

Lowercase

Trace the Letter. s

s s s s s s s s s s
s s s s s s s s s s
s s s s s s s s s s

UPPERCASE
Trace the Letter.
T
Lowercase
Trace the Letter.
t

UPPERCASE
Trace the Letter.
U
Lowercase
Trace the Letter.
u

UPPERCASE
Trace the Letter.
V
Lowercase
Trace the Letter.
v

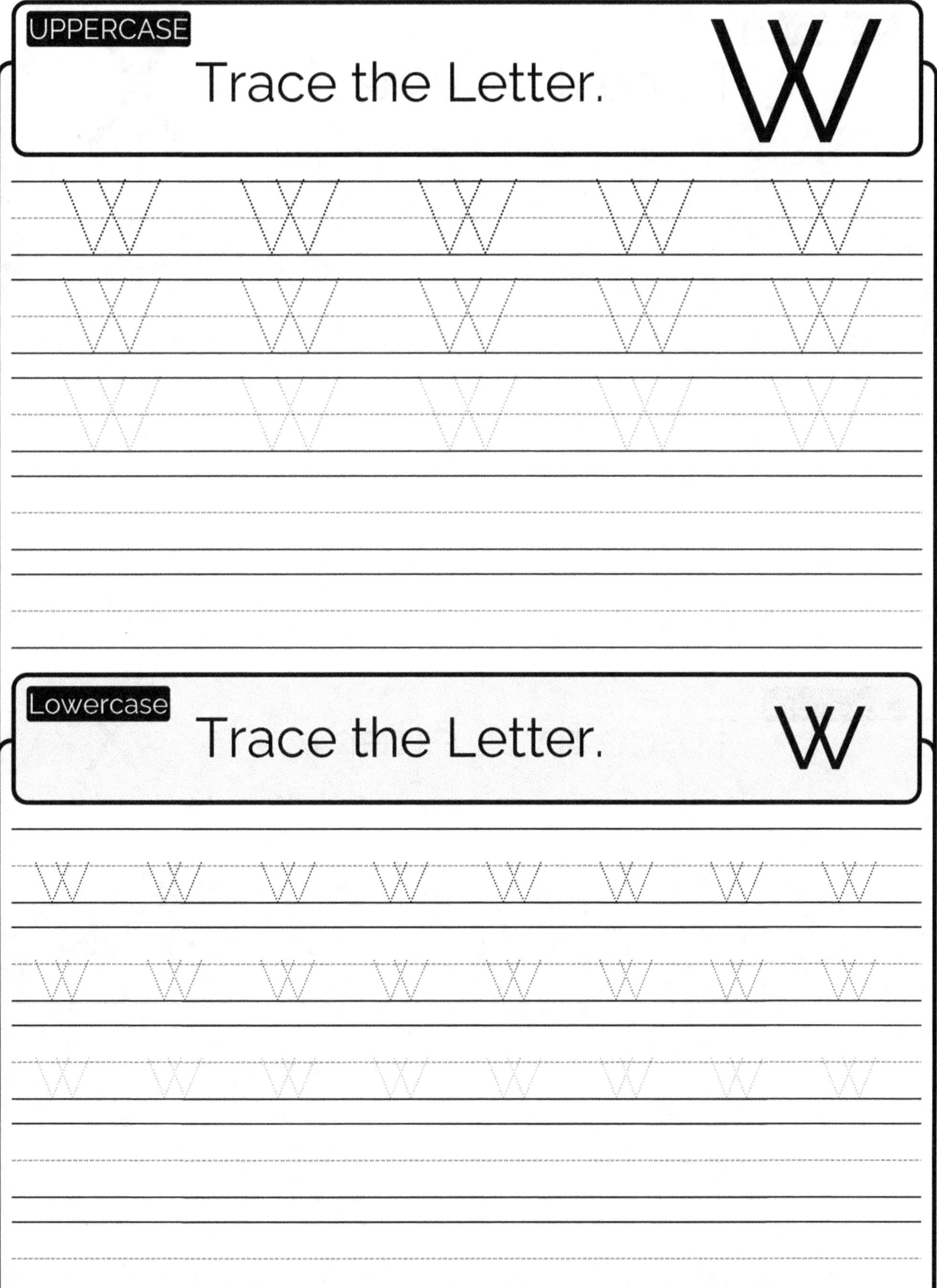
UPPERCASE
Trace the Letter.
W
Lowercase
Trace the Letter.
w

UPPERCASE

Trace the Letter. X

Lowercase

Trace the Letter. x

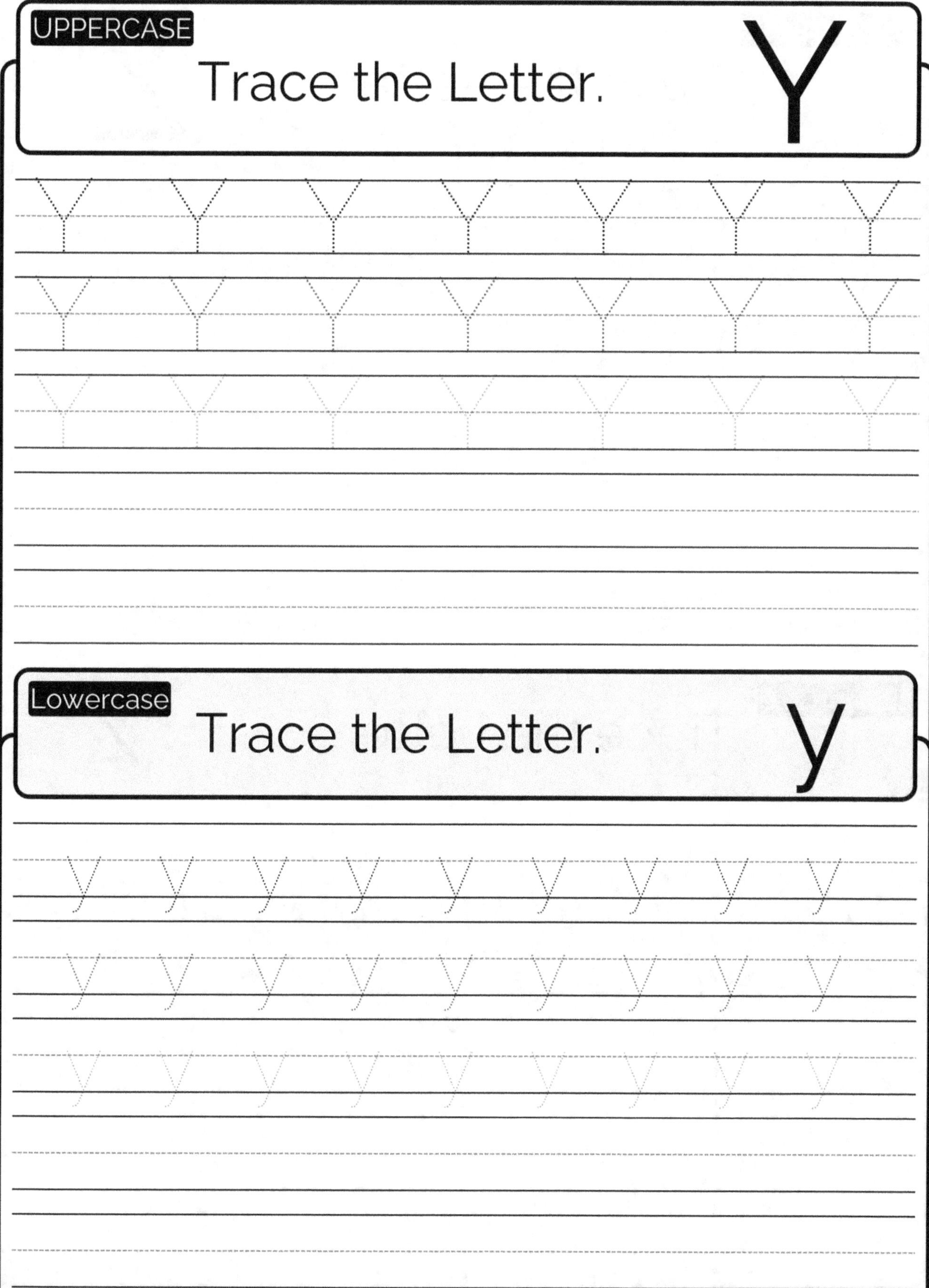
UPPERCASE
Trace the Letter.
Y
Lowercase
Trace the Letter.
y

UPPERCASE

Trace the Letter. Z

Lowercase

Trace the Letter. z

Number Tracing and Number Words Tracing

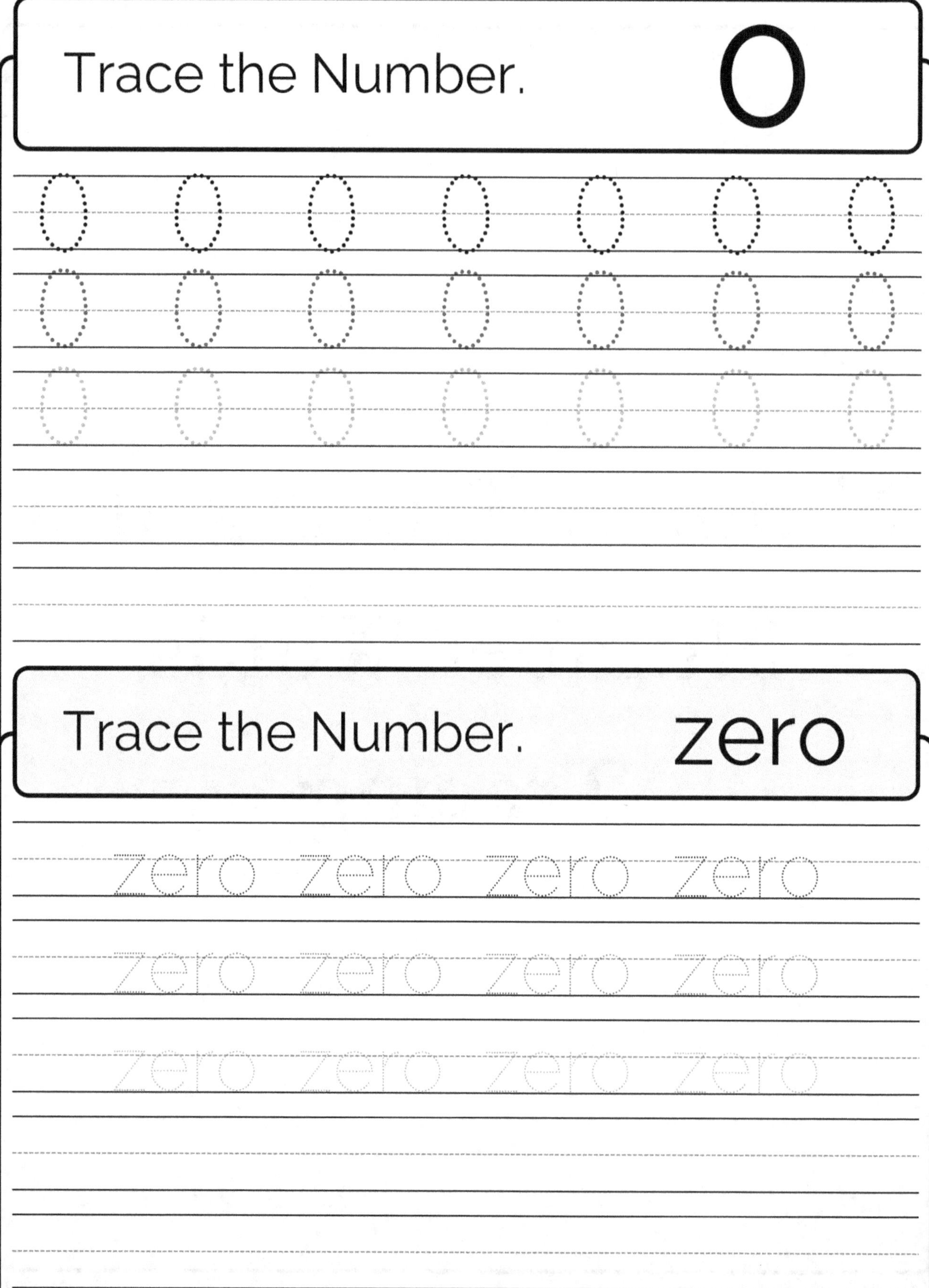
Trace the Number.
0
Trace the Number.
zero
zero zero zero zero
zero zero zero zero
zero zero zero zero

Trace the Number. 1

1 1 1 1 1 1 1

1 1 1 1 1 1 1

1 1 1 1 1 1 1

Trace the Number. one

one one one one one

one one one one one

one one one one one

Trace the Number. 2

2 2 2 2 2 2

2 2 2 2 2 2

2 2 2 2 2 2

Trace the Number. two

two two two two two

two two two two two

two two two two two

Trace the Number. 3

3 3 3 3 3 3 3

3 3 3 3 3 3 3

3 3 3 3 3 3 3

Trace the Number. three

three three three three

three three three three

three three three three

Trace the Number. 4

4 4 4 4 4 4 4

4 4 4 4 4 4 4

4 4 4 4 4 4 4

Trace the Number. four

four four four four four

four four four four four

four four four four four

Trace the Number. 5

5 5 5 5 5 5 5

5 5 5 5 5 5 5

5 5 5 5 5 5 5

Trace the Number. five

five five five five five

five five five five five

five five five five five

Trace the Number.
6
Trace the Number.
six

Trace the Number. 7

7 7 7 7 7 7 7

7 7 7 7 7 7 7

7 7 7 7 7 7 7

Trace the Number. seven

seven seven seven

seven seven seven

seven seven seven

Trace the Number. 8

8 8 8 8 8 8 8

8 8 8 8 8 8 8

8 8 8 8 8 8 8

Trace the Number. eight

eight eight eight eight

eight eight eight eight

eight eight eight eight

Trace the Number. 9

9 9 9 9 9 9 9
9 9 9 9 9 9 9
9 9 9 9 9 9 9

Trace the Number. nine

nine nine nine nine nine
nine nine nine nine nine
nine nine nine nine nine

Trace the Number. 10

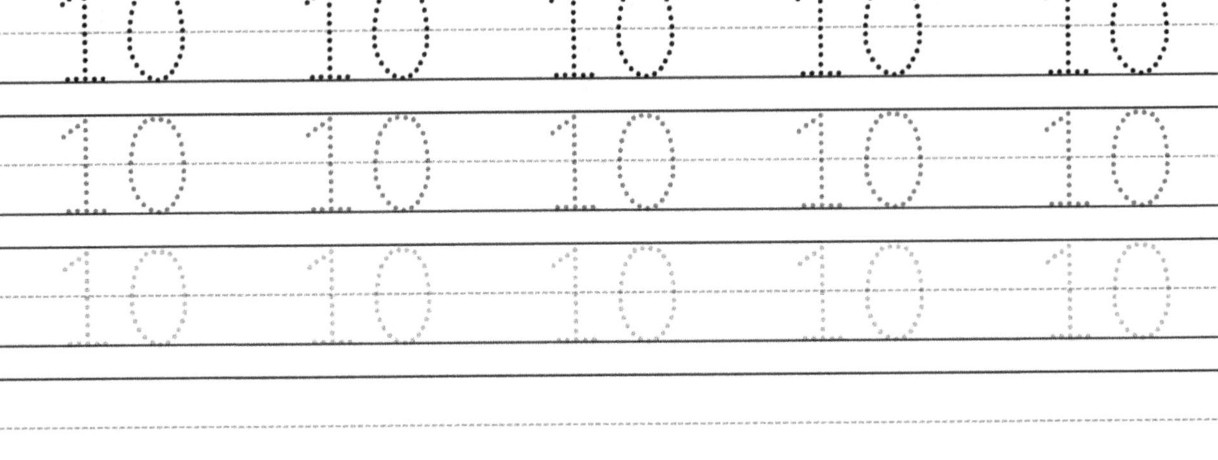

Trace the Number. ten

ten ten ten ten ten ten

ten ten ten ten ten ten

ten ten ten ten ten ten

Trace the Number. 11

11 11 11 11 11

11 11 11 11 11

11 11 11 11 11

Trace the Number. eleven

eleven eleven eleven

eleven eleven eleven

eleven eleven eleven

Trace the Number. 12

12 12 12 12 12

12 12 12 12 12

12 12 12 12 12

Trace the Number. twelve

twelve twelve twelve

twelve twelve twelve

twelve twelve twelve

Trace the Number. 13

13 13 13 13 13

13 13 13 13 13

13 13 13 13 13

Trace the Number. thirteen

thirteen thirteen thirteen

thirteen thirteen thirteen

thirteen thirteen thirteen

Trace the Number. 14

14 14 14 14 14

14 14 14 14 14

14 14 14 14 14

Trace the Number. fourteen

fourteen fourteen fourteen

fourteen fourteen fourteen

fourteen fourteen fourteen

Trace the Number. 15

15 15 15 15 15

15 15 15 15 15

15 15 15 15 15

Trace the Number. fifteen

fifteen fifteen fifteen

fifteen fifteen fifteen

fifteen fifteen fifteen

Trace the Number. 16

16 16 16 16 16

16 16 16 16 16

16 16 16 16 16

Trace the Number. sixteen

sixteen sixteen sixteen

sixteen sixteen sixteen

sixteen sixteen sixteen

Trace the Number. 17

17 17 17 17 17

17 17 17 17 17

17 17 17 17 17

Trace the Number. seventeen

seventeen seventeen

seventeen seventeen

seventeen seventeen

Trace the Number. 18

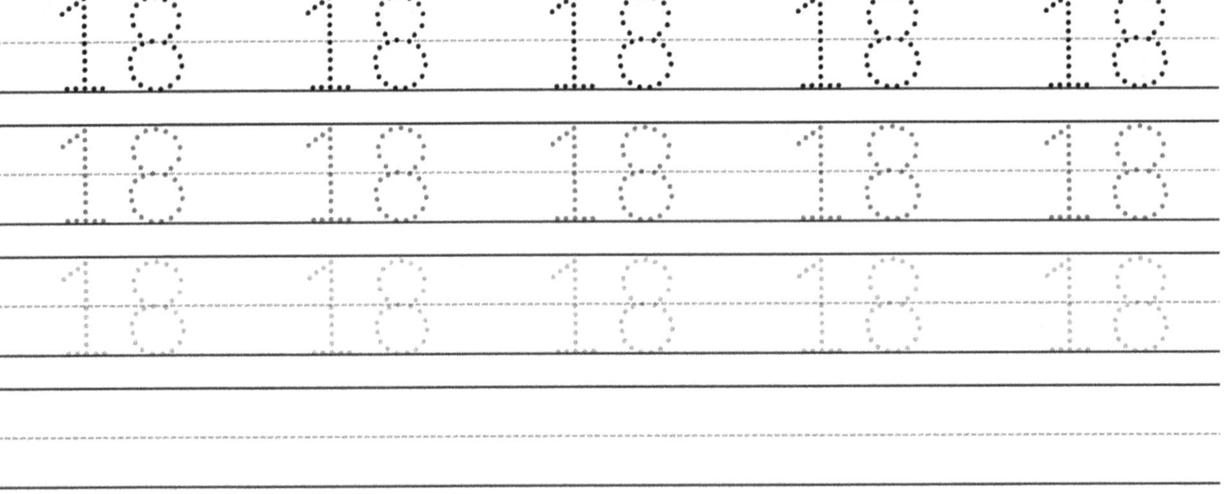

Trace the Number. eighteen

eighteen eighteen

eighteen eighteen

eighteen eighteen

Trace the Number. 19

19 19 19 19 19

19 19 19 19 19

19 19 19 19 19

Trace the Number. nineteen

nineteen nineteen

nineteen nineteen

nineteen nineteen

Trace the Number. 20

20 20 20 20 20
20 20 20 20 20
20 20 20 20 20

Trace the Number. twenty

twenty twenty twenty
twenty twenty twenty
twenty twenty twenty

Trace the Number. 21

21 21 21 21 21

21 21 21 21 21

21 21 21 21 21

Trace the Number. twenty-one

twenty-one twenty-one

twenty-one twenty-one

twenty-one twenty-one

Trace the Number. 22

22 22 22 22 22

22 22 22 22 22

22 22 22 22 22

Trace the Number. twenty-two

twenty-two twenty-two

twenty-two twenty-two

twenty-two twenty-two

Trace the Number. 23

Trace the Number. twenty-three

twenty-three twenty-three
twenty-three twenty-three
twenty-three twenty-three

www.ingramcontent.com/pod-product-compliance
Lightning Source LLC
Chambersburg PA
CBHW080300180726
47999CB00018B/2739